INSECTS UP CLOSE

Earwigs

by Patrick Perish

BLASTOFF! READERS

BELLWETHER MEDIA • MINNEAPOLIS, MN

Note to Librarians, Teachers, and Parents:

Blastoff! Readers are carefully developed by literacy experts and combine standards-based content with developmentally appropriate text.

Level 1 provides the most support through repetition of high-frequency words, light text, predictable sentence patterns, and strong visual support.

Level 2 offers early readers a bit more challenge through varied simple sentences, increased text load, and less repetition of high-frequency words.

Level 3 advances early-fluent readers toward fluency through increased text and concept load, less reliance on visuals, longer sentences, and more literary language.

Level 4 builds reading stamina by providing more text per page, increased use of punctuation, greater variation in sentence patterns, and increasingly challenging vocabulary.

Level 5 encourages children to move from "learning to read" to "reading to learn" by providing even more text, varied writing styles, and less familiar topics.

Whichever book is right for your reader, Blastoff! Readers are the perfect books to build confidence and encourage a love of reading that will last a lifetime!

This edition first published in 2018 by Bellwether Media, Inc.

No part of this publication may be reproduced in whole or in part without written permission of the publisher. For information regarding permission, write to Bellwether Media, Inc., Attention: Permissions Department, 5357 Penn Avenue South, Minneapolis, MN 55419.

Library of Congress Cataloging-in-Publication Data

Names: Perish, Patrick.
Title: Earwigs / by Patrick Perish.
Description: Minneapolis, MN : Bellwether Media, Inc., 2018. | Series:
   Blastoff! Readers. Insects Up Close | Audience: Ages 5-8. | Audience: K to
   grade 3. | Includes bibliographical references and index.
Identifiers: LCCN 2016055083 (print) | LCCN 2017004538 (ebook) | ISBN
   9781626176638 (hardcover : alk. paper) | ISBN 9781681033938 (ebook)
Subjects: LCSH: Earwigs–Juvenile literature.
Classification: LCC QL510 .P43 2018 (print) | LCC QL510 (ebook) | DDC
   595.7/39–dc23
LC record available at https://lccn.loc.gov/2016055083

Editor: Christina Leighton   Designer: Maggie Rosier

Printed in the United States of America, North Mankato, MN.

Table of Contents

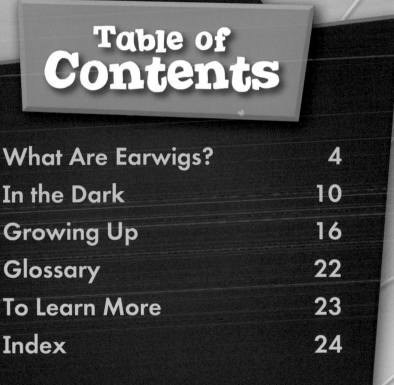

What Are Earwigs?

Earwigs are insects famous for their **pincers**. These scare off enemies.

pincer

Earwigs have hard, shiny bodies. They are often black, brown, or red.

Earwigs use **antennae** to smell and feel. They have wings but rarely fly.

← wing

antennae

wing

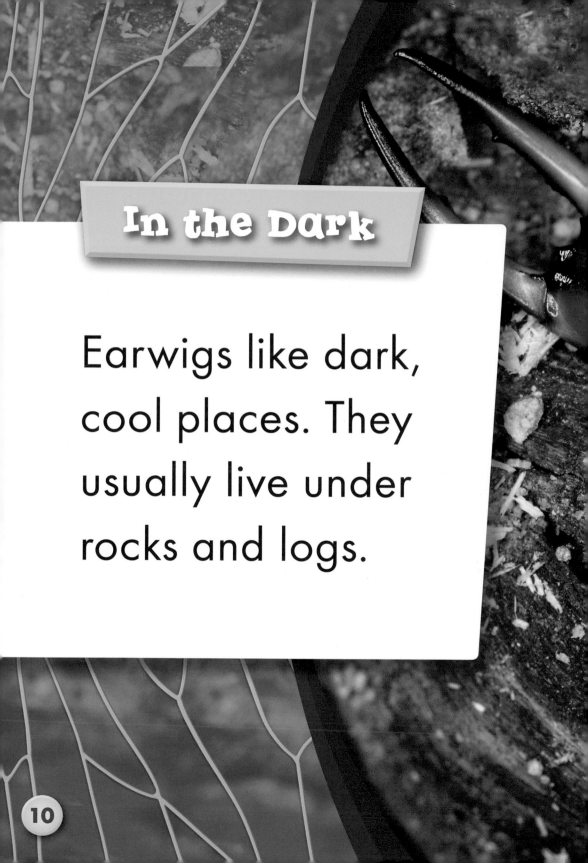

In the Dark

Earwigs like dark, cool places. They usually live under rocks and logs.

Earwigs rest during the day. These insects hunt at night.

13

Earwigs are not picky eaters. Most eat plants or small insects.

FAVORITE
FOOD:

marigolds

Growing Up

Female earwigs lay eggs and clean them. They also guard the eggs from **predators**.

EARWIG LIFE SPAN:

about 1 year

female earwig

eggs

17

The **nymphs** then **hatch** from eggs. The females feed them until they are strong.

nymphs

Nymphs **molt** as they grow. Soon, they are adults with big pincers!

**adult
earwig**

molting

Glossary

antennae

feelers connected to the head that sense information around them

nymphs

young insects; nymphs look like small adults without full wings.

hatch

to break out of an egg

pincers

hooks at the end of an earwig's body

molt

to shed skin for growth

predators

animals that hunt other animals for food

To Learn More

AT THE LIBRARY

Murawski, Darlyne, and Nancy Honovich. *Ultimate Bug-opedia: The Most Complete Bug Reference Ever.* Washington, D.C.: National Geographic, 2013.

Perish, Patrick. *Aphids.* Minneapolis, Minn.: Bellwether Media, 2018.

Zommer, Yuval. *The Big Book of Bugs.* New York, N.Y.: Thames & Hudson, 2016.

ON THE WEB

Learning more about earwigs is as easy as 1, 2, 3.

1. Go to www.factsurfer.com.

2. Enter "earwigs" into the search box.

3. Click the "Surf" button and you will see a list of related web sites.

With factsurfer.com, finding more information is just a click away.

Index

The images in this book are reproduced through the courtesy of: Anatolich, front cover, pp. 6-7; Ireneusz Waledzik, pp. 4-5; Awei, pp. 8-9; Antonio Clemens, pp. 10-11; David Peter Ryan, pp. 12-13, 22 (top left); WILDLIFE GmbH/ Alamy, pp. 14-15; Tim UR, p. 15; Graphic Science/ Alamy, pp. 16-17; Nature Production/ Nature Picture Library, pp. 18-19, 22 (center left); Artistas, pp. 20-21; blickwinkel/ Alamy, pp. 21, 22 (bottom left); IanRedding, p. 22 (top right); Colin J D Stewart, p. 22 (center right); Markus Hagenbucher, p. 22 (bottom right).